Getti...

THE NEW BUSINESS BUILDER'S CHECKLIST

☐ **USE YOUR OILS** Get passionate about the oils. Use them every day and start building your personal experience stories to share.

☐ **GET INVOLVED** Get connected with the person who enrolled you and ask to be added to their various groups and then be active. There are many educational groups both for the business and for oils!

☐ **EXPLORE THE VIRTUAL OFFICE** Log into your Virtual Office (VO) at www.youngliving.com and take time to explore.

☐ **SIGN UP FOR ER** Essential Rewards (ER) is the heart of the Young Living business. Make the business commitment of 100PV to start getting paid.

☐ **SET YOUR GOALS** Print out the compensation plan from your Virtual Office and set your goals based on your desired rank and income level.

☐ **GET EDUCATED** You only need to know 18 things: the 12 oils in the Premium Starter Kit, the diffuser, the samples of NingXia Red®, Thieves® Household Cleaner, and Thieves® Hand Purifier, the price, and your sign-up link.

☐ **SHARE YOUR STORIES** Do your best to share how essential oils help you and your family toward wellness.

☐ **BUILD YOUR TEAM** Do the business with people you love. Reach out to your favorite people first.

☐ **BE PERSISTENT** This will be the most fun, purpose-driven career you may ever have, and you will learn and grow in so many ways. Keep at it and be consistently persistent!

☐ **HAVE FUN** Enjoy everything this business has to offer, from the community to a healthier, clearer life-purpose.

YOUNG LIVING 2017 WORLDWIDE INCOME DISCLOSURE STATEMENT

Note: The following information is taken word-for-word from the "Young Living 2017 Worldwide Income Disclosure Statement" that may be found at www.youngliving.com/ids.

What are my earning opportunities?

This document provides statistical, fiscal data about the average member income and information about achieving various ranks within Young Living.

RANK	PERCENTAGE OF ALL BUSINESS BUILDERS[1]	MONTHLY INCOME[2]				AVERAGE YEARLY INCOME[3]	MONTHS TO ACHIEVE THIS RANK[4]		
		LOWEST	HIGHEST	MEDIAN	AVERAGE		LOW	AVE.	HIGH
DISTRIBUTOR	33.3%	$0	$725	$15	$26	$312	N/A	N/A	N/A
STAR	41.02%	$0	$932	$58	$75	$906	1	12	267
SENIOR STAR	15.66%	$2	$5,531	$193	$235	$2,819	1	19	255
EXECUTIVE	6.62%	$34	$13,210	$425	$502	$6,028	1	25	254
SILVER	2.55%	$229	$29,248	$1,698	$2,088	$25,059	1	32	252
GOLD	0.57%	$1,506	$48,630	$4,541	$5,666	$67,995	2	49	263
PLATINUM	0.18%	$4,375	$90,275	$11,057	$13,872	$166,468	5	58	243
DIAMOND	0.07%	$6,256	$163,387	$27,972	$35,348	$424,178	7	70	251
CROWN DIAMOND	0.01%	$28,492	$231,397	$53,589	$64,477	$773,724	16	85	258
ROYAL CROWN DIAMOND	0.02%	$50,770	$326,334	$132,828	$144,551	$1,734,606	17	97	230

YOUNG LIVING 2017 INCOME DISCLOSURE STATEMENT

The income statistics in this statement are for incomes earned by all worldwide active Business Builder members in 2017. An "active Business Builder" member is a member who has purchased at least 50 PV in the previous 12 months and has personally enrolled at least one person during the lifetime of the member account. The average annual income for all Business Builder members in this time was $3,321, and the median annual income was $684.

Note that the compensation paid to members summarized in this disclosure does not include expenses incurred by members in the operation or promotion of their business, which can vary widely and might include advertising or promotional expenses, product samples, training, rent, travel, telephone and internet costs, and miscellaneous expenses. The earnings of the members in this chart are not necessarily representative of the income, if any, that a Young Living member can or will earn through the Young Living Compensation Plan. These figures should not be considered as a guarantee or projections of your actual earnings or profits. Young Living does not guarantee any income or rank success.

1 Because a member's rank may change during the year, these percentages are not based on individual member ranks throughout the entire year, but are based on the average distribution of member ranks during the entire year. Business Builders are members who have personally enrolled at least one other person and does not include Preferred Customers.
2 A member's rank may change during the year, so these incomes are not based on individual member incomes throughout the entire year, but are based on earnings of all members qualifying for each rank during any month throughout the year.
3 This is calculated by multiplying the average monthly incomes by 12. These incomes include income earned from January 1, 2017 through December 31, 2017, but which was paid between February 2017 and January 2018.
4. These statistics include all historical ranking data for each rank and thus are not limited to people who achieved these ranks in 2017. Members who do not make at least on product purchase in the previous 12 months are considered inactive.

The Potential

THE INCREDIBLE INCOME POSSIBILITIES

One of the best strategies in this business is to build leaders. Helping others get to the rank of Silver, the first main leadership rank, should be one of your main goals. By creating other leaders in your organization, you will see your own paycheck skyrocket. A great strategy is to add Silvers, Golds, and Platinums to your "jewelry box," which, in turn, would give you more shares. A share is based on 1% of Young Living's total commissionable sales. The "jewelry box" describes the leaders in your organization and is 6 people across on your level 1 and 7 generations down.

Based on the Young Living compensation plan, you only need 6 business legs to get to their top rank of Royal Crown Diamond. Your goal would be to get each of your 6 legs to also get 6 legs. Then get all those 6 legs to get their 6 legs. You would continue this pattern down for 7 levels. The main goal would be to get each of those people to the rank of Silver or higher. For each Silver business person you have in your downline, you will get paid a Generational Bonus that averages out to be around $150 per share. If every one of your people were to hit Silver, 6 across and 7 down, you would make over 50 million dollars per month! And that is just your Generation Bonus. This does not include your unilevel commission or other commissions that you will also get on top of this.

The reality of every single business person in your downline hitting Silver is not realistic, but you will have people ranking higher than Silver in many cases. Most Royal Crown Diamonds can easily help 500 people to the rank of Silver or higher. If you only had 500 shares, you would be making $75,000 per month. It may be worth changing your plans for the next 2 years and working 80 hours a week so that 3-4 years from now you never have to work a normal 40-hour work week. Your life would literally change in a way you never thought possible. The Generation Leadership Bonus chart to the left is mind-blowing!

QUALIFICATIONS	DISTRIBUTOR	STAR	SENIOR STAR	EXECUTIVE
AVE. $ PER MO.[1]	$26	$75	$235	$502
PV	100	100	100	100
OGV		500	2,000	4,000
PGV				
LEGS X OGV				2 X 1,000

COMPENSATION	UNILEVEL COMMISSION PERCENTAGE			
LEVEL 1	8%	8%	8%	8%
LEVEL 2	5%	5%	5%	5%
LEVEL 3		4%	4%	4%
LEVEL 4			4%	4%
LEVEL 5				4%

UNDERSTANDING THE TERMINOLOGY

YL (YOUNG LIVING) How Young Living is commonly referred to.

PV (PERSONAL VOLUME) Total monthly volume of your personal orders.

OGV (ORGANIZATION GROUP VOLUME) Total monthly volume of your entire organization.

PGV (PERSONAL GROUP VOLUME) This is the total monthly volume of your personal group outside of your legs that rank you to Silver or higher.

LEGS X OGV This is the number of legs needed for that rank with the amount of volume needed in each leg.

VO (VIRTUAL OFFICE) Log into www.YoungLiving.com to access your VO.

ENROLLER The person who helped you purchase your kit.

SPONSOR The person who is directly above you. Sometimes this person is the same as your enroller.

DOWNLINE Your organization, including wholesale members, retail customers, and Business Builders.

UPLINE Those who are above you in the organization, such as your Enroller, Sponsor, and other Diamond and above leaders.

LEVEL The location of a business person or member within your organization.

RANK The current title you hold in Young Living as a Business Builder.

ER (ESSENTIAL REWARDS) Young Living's autoship reward program.

PSK (PREMIUM STARTER KIT) The best way to obtain wholesale membership.

[1] See Income Disclosure Statement on page 4.

The Plan

THE YOUNG LIVING COMPENSATION PLAN

SILVER	GOLD	PLATINUM	DIAMOND	CROWN DIAMOND	ROYAL CROWN DIAMOND
$2,088	**$5,666**	**$13,872**	**$35,348**	**$64,477**	**$144,551**
100	100	100	100	100	100
10,000	35,000	100,000	250,000	750,000	1,500,000
1,000	1,000	1,000	1,000	1,000	1,000
2 X 4,000	3 X 6,000	4 X 8,000	5 X 15,000	6 X 20,000	6 X 35,000

UNILEVEL COMMISSION PERCENTAGE

SILVER	GOLD	PLATINUM	DIAMOND	CROWN DIAMOND	ROYAL CROWN DIAMOND
8%	8%	8%	8%	8%	8%
5%	5%	5%	5%	5%	5%
4%	4%	4%	4%	4%	4%
4%	4%	4%	4%	4%	4%
4%	4%	4%	4%	4%	4%

GENERATION COMMISSION PERCENTAGES

SILVER	GOLD	PLATINUM	DIAMOND	CROWN DIAMOND	ROYAL CROWN DIAMOND
PERS. 2.5%	PERS. 2.5%	PERS. 2.5%	PERS. 2.5%	PERS. 2.5%	PERS. 2.5%
GEN 2: 3%	GEN 2: 3%	GEN 2: 3%	GEN 2: 3%	GEN 2: 3%	GEN 2: 3%
GEN 3: 3%	GEN 3: 3%	GEN 3: 3%	GEN 3: 3%	GEN 3: 3%	GEN 3: 3%
	GEN 4: 3%	GEN 4: 3%	GEN 4: 3%	GEN 4: 3%	GEN 4: 3%
		GEN 5: 3%	GEN 5: 3%	GEN 5: 3%	GEN 5: 3%
			GEN 6: 3%	GEN 6: 3%	GEN 6: 3%
				GEN 7: 3%	GEN 7: 3%
					GEN 8: 1%

BONUSES

FAST START BONUS
25% on new, personally-enrolled members' orders for the first three months. Maximum of $200.

START LIVING BONUS
One-time $25 bonus when your new, personally-enrolled member orders a Premium Starter Kit the same calendar month they enroll.

RISING STAR BONUS
Stars through Executives are eligible to earn shares based on 1% of Young Living's total monthly commissionable sales for building a strong foundation with 3 to 7 legs. See details on page 16 and in your Virtual Office.

GENERATION LEADERSHIP BONUS
Silvers and above qualify for this bonus and can make up the largest portion of your paycheck simply by building up other leaders! If you are a Silver leader, you will get generation leadership pay on every Silver or above leader in your downline.

ESSENTIAL REWARDS BENEFITS

EASY MONTHLY SHIPMENTS

Create your own monthly "Wellness Box".
Your favorite or new products come every month.

LOW MINIMUM

You only need 50PV per month to stay active in ER.

REDUCED SHIPPING

Get special reduced shipping options, plus the ability to join
YL GO and YL GO+ for even greater savings.

EARN FREE PRODUCT

Earn points toward future purchases.
Months 1 to 3 you'll get 10% back
Months 4 to 24 you'll get 20% back
Months 25+ you'll get 25% back
(1PV or point, usually equals $1)

EXCLUSIVE FREE BONUS OILS

Earn free exclusive oils at the 100PV & 190PV levels.
Plus, get more free promos at 250PV and 300PV.

EXCLUSIVE LOYALTY GIFTS

Earn gifts and get rewarded when you order for 3, 6, and 9 consecutive
months. Plus, you'll get an exclusive ER blend after your 12th month!

HASSLE FREE PROGRAM

Change your order, change your shipping date, or cancel all together!
You can use your points as soon as your second month enrolled in ER.

The Rewards

25% BACK

LEARN HOW TO GET 25% BACK ON YOUR MONTHLY ORDER!

Young Living truly honors their loyal customers. They want you to get the most out of their products, so they have created a great loyalty incentive program called ER or Essential Rewards. ER is Young Living's easy, automatic shipment program that allows you to order exactly what you want, when you want, while getting up to 25% back in points to spend on products you want to try or already love. Plus, enjoy special ER only exclusive oils starting at the 100PV level!

HOW TO GET STARTED ON ER

Log in to your wholesale membership account at www.YoungLiving.com under the Virtual Office. Select Essential Rewards in the left bar menu. Follow the instructions to sign up! Questions? Call 800-371-3515

GET ADDITIONAL FREE PROMOS

Each month, Young Living generously gives even more products to their loyal customers who order at specific PV level amounts. Incentive levels start at 100PV, 190PV, 250PV, and 300PV. These incentives are the most generous in the industry, and you will be amazed at the amount of free product you begin to receive when you maximize your Essential Rewards at the 300PV level! Plus, you can double up on these amazing promotions by placing a 300PV Essential Reward order *and* a 300PV Quick Order in the same month!

(Some ER only promotions will not apply for Quick Orders.)

The Purpose

SETTING YOURSELF UP FOR SUCCESS

Do what you love and the money will follow. Sadly, there may be a thousand things that you love to do that would not make you a dime. How do you figure out what you love to do that will also be both profitable and rewarding? There is no easy answer. If there was, we'd all be rich...and you wouldn't be reading this. The process you are about to work through will get you very close to your target, if not spot on. Successful people do the things unsuccessful people are unwilling to do. Be willing. Get ready to work. Get ready to dig deep into who you are and realistically find out what good things can come when you find your true purpose.

We hear this phrase all the time: "Do you know what your 'why' is?" The response in this business is often: "Because I love helping people," or, "Because I want to be with my family more." While yes, these may be part of your "why", it is not your systemic "why." "Why?" What a simple question; yet, what a loaded question. When it comes to your business and career, you may be truly stumped. Why is your "why" so important? Simply put, it dictates every area of your business: everything from startup, to identifying your market, to creating your brand, to how you sell, to how you create a buzz, and how you ultimately make money. Most importantly, it is what will keep you going when you want to quit. Your "why" is overwhelmingly important; yet, many business owners cannot answer this simple question without going in circles and rambling on.

Did you know you have a "why" even if you don't know how to articulate it? It usually stems from a belief system based on your true character: something rooted in your childhood, something you are on a mission to do, or something you are extremely passionate about. This belief becomes the foundation on which everything else is built. It is so important that it can also be considered part of your weakness as well.

There are usually deep, heavy emotions involved. These same emotions are tangled up in a person's buying patterns and reasonings. It is often said that your "why" should make you cry. Understand your "why" from an emotional standpoint, then market to people who feel the same way. You will have customers for life: customers who are true believers in your why, customers who tell every one of their friends to buy from you, or, better yet, become your most valued Business Builders alongside you. Can you see why your "why" is so incredibly important to you if you are a Business Builder?

Your "why" should be the good, the bad, and the ugly. Your "why" should be what drives you and what makes you, you. Below is a list of typical "whys" in the Young Living family. Can you pick out yours? Choose 2 or 3 and then personalize them with the underlying reason for why these areas fall into your greater "why" by exploring using the following method.

To get down to a deeper understanding of your core why, take a reason from below, or one that is important to you, and write it at the top of a piece of paper. Then ask yourself "Why is this my why?" and write down your answer. After you answer, ask yourself "why" again to the answer you gave. Continue to ask "why" until you get to a response that you cannot answer, then modify the question to "Why did that hurt me?" After the first modified question, end with the final question "Why does this matter to me today?" Below is an example to help you understand the process.

Example: To be financially free.
    Why? So I can stop worrying about the bills.
    Why? So I can focus more on relationships.
    Why? Because I grew up in an empty home.
    Why? My parents divorced and my mom had to go back to work.
    Why? Road Block! I do not know why my parents divorced.
        Note: When you get stuck, ask a slightly different "why" question.
    Why did that hurt me?
        I felt alone and often afraid.
    Why does this matter to me today?
        I never want my kids to ever feel that way.

FINDING YOUR WHY

TO FIND YOUR VOICE AND PURPOSE IN THIS WORLD.

TO HAVE DEEPER, MORE AUTHENTIC RELATIONSHIPS.

TO BE A PART OF A LARGER CAUSE OR PURPOSE.

TO BE A PART OF A LARGER COMMUNITY.

TO HELP FIND SOLUTIONS FOR OTHERS AND YOURSELF.

TO HAVE TIME FREEDOM OR TO HAVE FINANCIAL FREEDOM.

TO HELP OTHERS FIND TIME AND FINANCIAL FREEDOM.

TO HELP OTHERS DO THINGS CORRECTLY.

TO LIVE A MORE FULL AND HEALTHFUL LIFE.

TO HELP OTHERS LIVE A MORE FULL & HEALTHFUL LIFE.

FILL IN YOUR WHY STATEMENT HERE:

_____

BELIEF SETTING

Take a moment to write out your beliefs and how they may align with Young Living's. Commit to becoming a successfully passionate, true believer in yourself and the product you represent.

Product Beliefs: I know Young Living products are desirable because:
(List 3-5 reasons that are important to you.)

_____

_____

Company Beliefs: Young Living is a solid company because:
(List 3-5 reasons that you can stand behind.)

_____

_____

Personal Beliefs

My Strengths:

_____

_____

How will I become a better true believer in myself:

_____

_____

My Weaknesses:

_____

_____

How will I strengthen these areas:

_____

_____

The Passion

HOW TO BECOME A TRUE BELIEVER

The thing about doing the business side is that you need to be a true believer. Think about it…would you buy anything from anyone who was ho-hum about what they were selling? One of the largest contributing factors to our buying habits is because someone else was incredibly passionate about it. It is your job to be a true believer. What exactly does that mean? Some might connect it to fanaticism; others might attribute it to religion. With regard to your business, look at it as true success. With most things in life, our beliefs motivate our actions, good or bad. We base our lives on certain convictions we believe to be true. These convictions either help us or hinder us. The goal, then, is to have a belief system in place that helps us. Outlined below are three areas to consider on the path to becoming a true believer in your Young Living career.

BELIEF IN THE PRODUCT

In order to do your job well, you must truly believe in Young Living products. People are going to pay their hard-earned cash for it. You must believe so wholeheartedly in what you offer that you have no doubt in your mind that people will want and need it. Know that the price is unbeatable because the product is so amazing. Each bottle is worth its weight in gold!

BELIEF IN THE COMPANY

Young Living Essential Oils has standards, ethics, and philosophies by which it operates. These standards, ethics, and philosophies should closely mirror your personal ones. If you don't know exactly what they are, take a moment to identify them. Check out www.youngliving.com and www.seedtoseal.com to further your understanding.

BELIEF IN YOURSELF

This is the most important belief. This is the reason you will succeed or fail. Many people were brought up in a world of "I can't." We are full of excuses. But when it comes right down to it, 99% of the time you can, or could have, if you'd have only tried. The best attitude to instill in yourself and those around you is: *I can do anything I put my mind to as long as I am willing to do the work.* If you believe in yourself and are realistic about the effort you must put forth, anything is possible. Nations have been created, life-changing inventions have been made, diseases have been cured, and people's lives have been saved because of a single individual's willingness to try. Believe in yourself and believe that you can do whatever it takes to make your career a success.

The Team

SETTING UP A SUCCESSFUL STRATEGY

Young Living allows you the ability to place anyone you sign up under someone else as their sponsor in your downline; you remain the enroller. Your goal is to place them strategically into your downline for the greatest benefit. Setting a strategy in place beforehand is a good place to start. Note: as the enroller, you are their main contact person. You get the kit sale commission and any unilevel commission moving forward. The sponsor gets the benefit of unilevel commission plus a bump in their OGV, and you build your team to help you reach the next rank. Win-win!

There are three ways to place someone. The first is at sign up. You use your member number as the enroller number, and the member number of the person you would like to place them under as their sponsor number. You may easily create a link under Link Builder under Member Services in your Virtual Office. You may also move anyone you enroll within the first 5 days by calling in the move or by using the online chat feature. You may change the enroller and/or the sponsor very easily in this first 5 days. If you need to make a change after 5 days, you have 20 days to do it via email by sending your move request to resolutions@youngliving.com. You only get to move someone once after their initial sign up placement.

The simple loophole in this is to strategically consider where you want them in your organization when you sign them up. For instance, if you were going to sell a kit today, you would consider that person and where you want them before you sign them up. That way you can adjust the sign-up link so they are placed where you want them from the beginning. Should you choose to move them, you have 21 days to do so. Once the 21 days have passed or you have moved them one time after enrollment, they will stay with that enroller/sponsor. The only way to change their spot would be to get a three upline approval form or for them to go inactive for 6 months and pay a small fee to change their sponsor. This is why it is important to carefully consider where you want them when you sign them up.

Place people based on two factors: they may be a loyal customer with no intention of doing the business; or, they may have the potential to be a Business Builder. You will want to place Business Builders on your level 1 if you do not have all 6 spots filled. If you have all your level 1 spots filled, you may start building on your level 2. If you think they will be only a loyal customer, it is best to place them as far down as your level 5 so you can help build the businesses of the most people on your team. Placing someone below your level 6 is not a smart strategy because you do not make unilevel commission past level 5. Placing a customer on your level 3, 4, or 5 will help the overall OGV of everyone above that person. This is a great way to help support and build leaders! Don't worry about the small amount of unilevel commission difference between a level 1 and level 2 or 3. In the long run, this will not matter as much as you think it might.

It is not the best strategy to place anyone under someone who is *not* doing the business, unless they are a blood relative. In order for a Business Builder team member to qualify to become a sponsor of a person you are placing under them, they should have four specific things in place. These are not hard and fast rules, but they will help give you clarity on when and where to place someone.

BUSINESS BUILDER QUALIFICATIONS

1. They are doing 100PV minimum per month.
2. They are on Essential Rewards.
3. They have personally told you they want to do the business.
4. They are *actually* doing the business.
   "Doing the business" means they sell 1-2 kits per month, actively participate in the business groups, and work weekly toward income-producing activities.

BUILDING A STRATEGIC TEAM

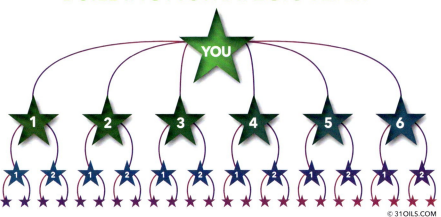

© 31OILS.COM

The key to understanding the above diagram is to remember that the stars are your Business Builders and not your customers. You will inevitably have many customers on your level 1, 2, 3, and all the way down even to level 100 and beyond as you continue to work this business. Your focus is what many people in Young Living call their "jewelry box." These are your Business Builders that are 6 across (in some cases 7 across) and 5 down. When qualifying for the higher ranks, you would look down to your 8th generation as well. Your focus should be helping those closest to you get to Silver and show them how to duplicate the process. The diagram shows six Business Builders on your level 1, plus your next two levels with 2 Business Builders on each. They each eventually need six, but two is the best starting point. Your starting point strategy is to find 2 Business Builders and have them also find 2 Business Builders and continue to duplicate the process. Once you find 2, continue to be on the look out for your number 3-6 level 1 Builders. This is what it looks like to set up a successful strategy with Young Living Essential Oils!

THE RISING STAR BONUS

Young Living Essential Oils® wants to help their distributors succeed! They have implemented a bonus only available for new Business Builders, from Star, to Senior Star, to Executive. It is called the Rising Star Bonus. While most people in direct sales haphazardly build their businesses hoping things will fall into place, Young Living has outlined, from the very beginning of your journey, exactly what you need to do to set up a strong business foundation. Business Builders who are eligible earn shares based on 1% of all Young Living's monthly commissionable sales.

Qualifications to Earn the Rising Star Bonus:

1. Paid as a rank of Star, Senior Star, or Executive.
2. Have an Essential Rewards order of 100 PV.
3. Build legs based on the following steps, in this specific order:

Step 1: For one share – have 3 legs each, with a minimum OGV of 300 with each main person at 100PV on Essential Rewards.

Step 2: For two additional shares (3 shares total) – have step 1 in place and add 2 more legs. All 5 legs must be on ER with a minimum of 100PV each. 2 legs must be at 500 OGV or more, and 3 legs must be at 300 OGV or more.

Step 3: For 3 additional shares (6 shares total) – have step 1 and 2 in place and add 2 more legs, for a total of 7 legs. All 7 legs must be on ER with a minimum of 100PV each. 2 legs must be at 1,000 OGV or more, 2 legs must be at 500 OGV or more, and 3 legs must be at 300 OGV or more.

Building a Team

HOW TO FIND BUSINESS BUILDERS

Finding Business Builders is the most important part of doing this business, and duplicating the process is key. For most it seems natural to let people join the business side organically. This is mostly true, but you may be overlooking one simple fact: many people who sign up to be a wholesale member of Young Living most likely have no idea there is an incredible business side. Shift your thinking. When you sign up a new member, introduce the business in a casual way, but *do* introduce it. Consider the blessing this business is for you and that your customers may need the same blessing.

Of course, always lead with the product first, but the business should be a close second. Share passionately with them how much they will fall in love with the products and once they start using them, they are not going to be able to keep their mouths shut about how amazing they all are. Mention, almost in passing, that when a friend of theirs wants to get their own kit, they will get a paycheck of $50-$100 or more. When they understand the major value and benefits of the products, they will perk up when they hear potential paycheck numbers. The goal is to get the light bulb in their head to turn on. Drip on them. If you fire-hose them, they will feel like they are being sold something they may not be ready for. If you drip on them, they will feel like they figured it out on their own and the light bulb *will* go off! Allowing your new member to gain ownership over their buying process will go a long way in your duplication process.

If you are intentional about introducing the business to your friends and customers, you will get more business people. What should you be looking for when trying to find business people? People who are introverts and people who are extroverts. People who are confident and people who are shy. People who have huge networks and people who have small networks. Basically, all types of people, yet most importantly, people who are motivated to do more, find freedom, and help others. You can inspire people with your own story, but *their* story is the only thing that will motivate them to skyrocket. Listen to your customers. Find out their desires, needs, and wants. Share with them the freedom this opportunity can bring. Don't keep it all to yourself; be generous!

On a separate piece of paper, write the names of the people you would like to see join your team. Claim them. This is a good time to vision cast; make a plan based on your own dreams and desires. Put the people down that you want to do life with. These are the people you will go to Convention with, travel to the farms with, and go on leadership cruises with. Many choose to add close family and best friends, while others will add people they know would enjoy this type of business and love helping people. It is best to choose a little of both! The most important spots to focus on in the beginning are your level 1 and level 2 Business Builders. Once you write them all down, meet up with each one individually and tell them your story. Show them your passion. Ask what their long term dreams are. Ask them if they want to come along and join you on the journey!

The Colors

THE FOUR PERSONALITY COLORS

When you start to dig deeper into the art of communicating with people in order to build a relationship, you will start to realize that each person has a specific language pattern that will help or hinder you from communicating with them. These personalities are broken down into four colors: yellow, green, red, and blue. No one is 100% any color. You may find your personality is mostly one color with variations found in the other three, or you will find that you seem to have a little from each type. That is perfectly fine. Your personality will change as you grow, but your core personality typically stays the same. Read the following descriptions to find out where you fit best and how to communicate with the other colors. To take the color test go to www.31oils.com/thecolortest.

YELLOWS = YELLOW LABS

Yellow personalities are like yellow Labrador Retrievers. They are your best friend, very loyal, caring, and loving. They desire to help anyone whenever they can. They often help others even at their own expense. Yellows enjoy volunteering for and supporting a good cause and are generally peace-loving individuals. They like following systems and will readily look to ethical leaders. They are humble and happy people who enjoy small social gatherings where intimacy can be built. Yellows have excellent relationship building skills and make great hostesses. They are sometimes overly sensitive and can take rejection personally. Yellows can easily bottle up anger or frustration, only to erupt later. They are people-pleasers who aim to keep the peace, so they often avoid conflict or back off when there is a possibility of confrontation or an argument. Yellows appreciate people who use a softer tone of voice and are wary of people who talk fast. They enjoy conversation that is give and take without being rushed. Yellows desire others to be honest and authentic and give them lots of encouragement in areas they feel they need help with. Show a Yellow that they can accomplish their goals and cheer them on. The best way to communicate with a Yellow is to show them how they will be helping people to improve their lives.

GREENS = GREEN GRASS

Greens like all the details. When considering a blade of grass that is often over looked, greens like to know all about that blade of grass; how it got there, how it works, why it works that way, how it affects them, etc. Greens love to analyze everything. They love graphs, charts, and statistics. Greens will research all the pros and cons before making decisions. They are perfectionists who love precision, but are also known for having analysis paralysis. Greens do not work well under pressure, and often take a very long time to complete tasks. They do not like change and appreciate order in their life. Greens appreciate people who give them time to come to a conclusion on their own rather than force them to make a decision. They like people to point them in the right direction. Greens want an honest, direct, helpful, and true approach with all the details. Show a Green graphs, charts and scientific studies, and you will have a happy Green.

REDS = RED FIRE

Reds are like fires because they are hot with lots of sparks. Reds are considered very passionate and driven. They can be fierce and always demand attention, but also can bring light and truth. Reds are natural leaders but also can get too aggressive or immovable in their decisions. They are often visionaries who like to take risks and love being challenged. Reds will be honest at all times, telling the truth even if it hurts. They are great self-starters and are known to take initiative in leadership roles. Reds like to get things done and have great follow-through on projects. They are known to feel superior to others thinking that their way is the right way and can come off as arrogant. Reds are often motivated by money and a desire to understand what is in it for them. They can be very selfish and concerned only with how they look to others. Reds often change direction too fast and will make snap decisions without thinking it through. Their competitive edge can get in the way of being a team player. Reds appreciate people who get right to the point and tell them how something will benefit them. They like others to give them lots of compliments and thrive on people asking them for their opinion. You can recruit a Red by asking them for advice on how they would run your business if they were you. Indirect suggestion works best with Reds. Give them space to do it their own way.

BLUES = BLUE SKY

Blues are the talkers and dreamers. They often have their head in the clouds and love to party. Everything is "sky's the limit" so they like to have lots of fun and are always on the go. They love to travel and thrive on meeting new people. They are great collaborators and are motivated by fun rewards like traveling, recognition, and gifts. Blues are very passionate and will seek out new and exciting adventures. They love the outdoors and have a general love for life. Blues can often forget that they are dominating the conversation, so it is sometimes hard to get a word in. They can also get so involved in what they are doing creatively that they forget what time it is and are often late to appointments. They are easily distracted and get easily bored. Blues have a tendency toward internal depression. They want everyone to view them as the happy-go-lucky person they portray, but often the stress of life builds up and they can be riddled with internal turmoil without anyone knowing. Blues appreciate people who give them lots of encouragement. It is best for people to communicate by using stories to hold their attention. Show a Blue the potential for meeting new people, the travel opportunities, and the incredible community your team has to offer. Blues love energetic group cultures. If there is nothing exciting or fun about your meetings or gatherings, they simply won't show up.

The Activities

STEPS TO SHARING THE RIGHT WAY

BECOME THE OIL LADY OR OIL GUY

Use the product all the time! Learn, grow, use, believe. Once you really understand that these oils are worth their weight in gold, it is quite impossible *not* to share how great they are with everyone around you. If everyone in your world does not know you use and sell essential oils, then you are doing something wrong. Carry oils with you at all times.

BUSINESS TRAINING

Take advantage of any and all training resources that your team and Young Living has to offer. If you are unaware of these resources, ask your enroller. If they do not know, log into your Virtual Office and see who your leaders are under your Profile section and contact them directly.

EDUCATIONAL TRAINING

Educate yourself and, in turn, educate your friends and customers. Having an online group dedicated to education goes a lot further than one that promotes what products you are trying to sell. If you like hosting parties, make it a fun, educational workshop. Do simple DIY oil projects. These parties are often called "Make & Takes". You do not need to be a perfect presenter! You only need to have fun and be passionate!

RELATIONSHIP BUILDING

People don't care how much you know until they know how much you care. Talk to people. Engage in their life outside of oils. Get to know new people and reconnect with those you already know. Care for them in a real way and be authentic.

STORY TELLING

Share stories about how you use oils and how they work for you and your family. You cannot share stories unless you use the product. Start with your first set of oils from the Premium Starter Kit and find out everything they do. Use them often on yourself so you have more stories to share. Get excited about learning new ways to improve your life by trying new products. Enjoy the simple blessing you will be to others by sharing your personal testimonials.

STRATEGY

Start mapping out your business strategy. Each month, determine who on your team is doing the business and know what their goals are. Keep a running list of people you would like to see join your team and those who may be really into their oils who may want to check out the business, too. Make your main goal at the beginning of your team building to find at least 2 people who may want to do the business with you and make them your Level 1 Business Leaders. This is the most important first step to your strategy to build a strong foundation. From there, you will want to continue to build until you have 6 strong Level 1 Business Leaders and each of those have at least 2 strong Business Builders under them.

SHARE A DROP

People tend to not know what to do with a gifted essential oil if you give them a full bottle or even a smaller bottle. It may end up stuffed in a drawer, never to be used. It is best to share with them one drop for something specific, rather than give them a full sample. Some oils to consider carrying with you for others are Stress Away™, PanAway® and Peppermint, for instant gratification.

SELL A KIT & GET PEOPLE ON ER

Selling Premium Starter Kits and getting people on Essential Rewards is the heart of the business. Set a monthly goal of double the number of kits you want to sell. Hold a minimum of 1-2 classes or workshops per month for both existing and new customers. If classes are not an option for you, then try online sharing and classes, one on one meet-ups, or even over the phone sharing. Look into joining a local street fair, farmers market, or health fair. There are countless ways to connect with new customers, so stretch your thinking. Your monthly goal should be to HELP 5. This is Young Living's best way for you to grow your business. Focus on helping 5 total people per month either by helping a new person buy a kit or helping a current customer enroll in Essential Rewards. When it comes to Essential Rewards, always keep in mind that your current customers are already sold on the product so the best time to get them enrolled in Essential Rewards is during the membership sign up process. It is your job to help them make the most of their money. Essential Rewards is the best loyalty program in the industry, with up to 25% back in free product plus amazing bonus products at various levels. Be passionate about the product and the rewards. Your passion will pour over onto them and hopefully will become their passion!

The 101 Class

HOW TO TEACH A BASIC 101 OIL CLASS

• Invite 4 times as many people as you would like to attend.
• Personally invite each person 1-2 weeks before the event.
  Do not send out a group email or group text.
• If they say they can come, leave out some information so you
  can have multiple connection points.
• Example connection points:
  ~ 4 days before, ask if they have any friends they would like to bring
    so you can have enough supplies for the group DIY project.
  ~ 2 days before, give them your address.
  ~ 1 day before, share that you are very excited about the party and
    ask them what their favorite color is (you can use this info to pick
    up some ribbon for the make and take for them to personalize it).
    Also ask if they can come 15 minutes early to help you set up.
    Give them a job and they are sure to not cancel.
  ~ Day of, let them know your door will be unlocked and to come on in.

THE SIMPLE 101 CLASS OUTLINE

~ *DIY Project Prelude:* Do a simple DIY project first as an ice-breaker. This will allow guests who arrive late to not miss the important things. Examples of DIY projects: Bath salts, Lavender hand lotion, or a Stress Away™ rollerball. Make them simple and all under $2-3 each. See page 30-31 for easy recipes using the PSK.

~ *No DIY Project Prelude:* Start the class with an open Q&A based on issues they would like support with. Help them to think of things by giving examples such as, "Do you need help with more energy at 3pm, or do you want help to support a more restful night's sleep?" Answer as many questions as you can while waiting for all the guests to arrive. Don't waste this time waiting for people. Of course normal social chitchat should happen, but realistically, use your time well. Start individual conversations with people as they come in, but do it in a group setting.

1. Gather your guests to the main presentation room. Formally welcome your guests and share a little about you and why you got into oils. Tell a short 3-5 minute testimonial about how oils have changed and enhanced your life.

2. Share several statistics from "The Statistics" on page 25.

3. Briefly introduce the starter kit. Share the price up front: both retail and wholesale.

4. Cover the basics of EOs in under 2 minutes. Sample: Essential oils are the volatile fragrant molecules in a plant that actively work to help promote systematic regulation and healthful modification of plant cells. These oils can work in much the same way for us. There are three ways to use essential oils: aromatically, topically, and internally. It takes 20 minutes for an essential oil to reach every cell in your body from the time

you apply them. There are around 40-100 trillion cells in our bodies, and one drop of essential oil contains over 40 million trillion molecules! This means every single cell in our body, in 20 minutes, is covered by at least 400,000 essential oil molecules.

5. Go over each oil in the PSK (see section on The Oil Basics) and pass it around as you discuss it so everyone can smell it. Try to get this down to about 20 minutes. Share 2-3 ways each oil is commonly used. This is the best time to tell your stories. Get excited about each oil. Build value with each passing oil. Remember, they need all of them. Don't pass over an oil in the kit because you do not know what to say about it. Educate yourself and get excited about them all.

6. Share why Young Living is different (Seed to Seal®) from all other brands. This is a great time to do a smell test using 3 oils (optional). Use peppermint from Young Living and two other companies, such as a major competitor and one that you can buy in a grocery store. All of them should be covered up so you do not disclose who the other brands are. This becomes a wonderful opportunity to share the difference between how oils are processed and why the smell can help you know the difference. Share the what fractional distillation is. Young Living oils always smell more earthy, while the others will have a sweeter smell. You can use the full script in the Live Well with Young Living app or get the Live Well mini class book at 31oils.com/live-well.

7. Go over what is in the kit, the retail price first (over $400), and then the wholesale membership price ($165).

8. Share the custom kit too. See "The Custom Kit" on page 32-33.

9. Go over that *when* they buy (not *if* they buy), they will get access to your private online education groups and also a custom oil map, if you choose to do one. (See the book, *French Aromatherapy* by Jen O'Sullivan for details on Oil Mapping.)

10. Go over how they can buy single oils as a retail customer, but then go over why that is not the smartest move. Lead with Frankincense and PanAway®. Those two oils will cost them $87.83 before tax and shipping, when for another $77.17 they will get 10 more necessary oils and a diffuser that retail for over $400. This will help showcase the difference and they will make the best choice accordingly.

11. Ask happily and in a heartfelt way if anyone would like to buy a kit, host a party, or join your team! Share briefly what the business has done for you and how you would love to help them host their first party. Then tell them, "First things first, I want you to fall head over heels in love with your oils, so let's order your kit!" Ask for the sale. Don't just wrap it up and say goodnight. Don't peter out with a Q&A session. Walk them through the process step by step together, all at the same time.

12. End on time and don't forget to laugh and have fun. Do not do anything over-produced at parties. Simple, pretty, and fun is best! Have fun, and don't go crazy stressing yourself out about it. The more over the top you make your classes, the harder it will be for others to envision themselves doing it. You want people to say, "Wow, I could totally do this!"

13. For those who did not buy a kit, find out why and then follow up. Be friendly, yet persistent. Continue to share your love and passion for the oils and why you know they will love them too!

14. Do it again and again and again! Practice makes perfect, and while classes do not need to be perfect, your nerves will be more settled the more you host.

OIL QUALITY

AUTHENTIC These essential oils are 100% pure throughout the bottle. There are no added synthetics or other species of oils . They are also the correct species, meaning what the labels says is what is in the bottle. Many companies will label it as one species only to use a less expensive similar species in the actual bottle. These usually are not from fractional distillation methods and are absolutely not rectified.

MANIPULATED Perfumers are often hired by essential oil companies to help make the final product smell more pleasing and less earthy. They will add very small amounts of one or two other species of oil to enhance the smell of the main oil. A common example of this, as shared by Dr. Cole Woolley, is Lavender oil with 1% Geranium and 1% Roman Chamomile as a final manipulated oil to create a more floral scented oil. They will also use this technique to rectify oils to make them smell similar batch to batch. Companies also take away some of the heavier molecules using fractional distillation.

PERFUME Often you will see an essential oil labeled as "pure" when they are not. The company has used a percentage of pure essential oil and usually a smaller percentage of synthetic to enhance the smell. A couple examples of this, as shared by Dr. Cole Woolley, are Lavender with 5% linalyl acetate for a more floral aroma or Peppermint with 1% ethyl vanillin to give it a more "candy cane" aroma.

SYNTHETIC These "essential oils" are not actually essential oils at all. Because there are no labeling regulations on the term "essential oil," full synthetic oils are able to be labeled as pure and sold to unsuspecting consumers. A couple examples of this, as shared by Dr. Cole Woolley, are 90% of "natural wintergreen" sold on the market is actually 100% synthetic, and linalyl acetate added to alcohol then labeled as pure Lavender. Companies do this to increase profit margins.

The Statistics

STATS TO USE WHEN EDUCATING

Many of the chemicals found in our personal care products are toxic and wreak havoc on our bodies. Of the 2,938 chemicals tested, 884 are toxic, 146 can cause tumors, 218 can cause reproductive complications, 778 can cause acute toxicity, 314 can cause biological mutations, and 376 can cause skin and eye irritations. *Source: United States House of Representatives Report from the National Institute of Occupational Safety and Health (NIOSH), 1989.*

Stay-at-home moms and women who work from home are 54% more likely to die from cancer than women who don't work from home. *Source: 15 year Toronto Indoor Air Conference of 1990 study.*

The EPA stated as of their 1980 report that there are 70,000 chemicals that have been introduced into our environment since 1950. It has been also stated that it is estimated there are 3,000 new chemicals (see next statistic) introduced every year. This would double the number as claimed in 1980. *Source: EPA, "Your Guide to the Environmental Protection Agency," December 1980.*

"It is generally understood that the number of chemical compounds currently recognized in the United States exceeds 3 million, and approximately 3,000 new ones are being added each year." *Source: "Technologies and Management Strategies for Hazardous Waste Control," March 1983 by the United States Congress, Office of Technology Assessment.*

To date, the EPA has reviewed over 36,000 chemicals. This is a small amount compared to the over 100,000 chemicals in use today. *Source: Chemical Safety Facts: "Debunking the Myths: Chemicals and Testing for Safety."*

There was an average of 150,000 emergency room treated injuries associated with household chemicals from 1997-2004. *Source: National Electronic Injury Surveillance System, 1997-2004 as stated in the 2007 Hazard Screening Report - Home and Family Maintenance Products – Household Chemicals by the Consumer Product Safety Commission.*

"Each year, 90,000 children are treated in emergency departments for unintentional poisonings. Nearly 40 die. 90% of poison incidents happen at home." *Source: The United States Consumer Product Safety Commission "Poison Prevention Poster," 2013.*

"Cosmetics intended for retail sale must have a list of ingredients on the label. The list does not have to include flavor, fragrance, or trade secret ingredients." *Source: The American Cancer Society, based on the FDA regulations of cosmetics.*

LAVENDER

Lavender is a single species oil and is one of the most well-known and well-loved essential oils. It is commonly referred to as the "Swiss Army Knife" of oils. There is more synthetic Lavender on the market than the real thing, and Young Living's is the purest you can get. Young Living offers Lavender in the normal line as well as the Vitality line for consumption, but they are the exact same oil inside.

Common Uses: Vitality – cardiovascular, immunity, respiratory, and nervous system. Normal – calming emotions, skin support, skin smoothing and soothing, seasonal support, hair strength, sleep support.

Best Practice: Vitality – add a couple drops to a capsule for daily support. Normal – diffuse during the day for better focus. Diffuse at night for a more restful night's sleep. Add a few drops to your daily face cream and serum. Add several drops to water in a spray bottle to mist over a pillow or to freshen a room.

FRANKINCENSE

Frankincense is a single species oil and has been traded around the Middle East for over 5,000 years. The tree is cut, and the sap/resin that slowly oozes out of the tree and dries is what is collected and steam distilled. It is offered both in the normal and Vitality line through Young Living. They are the exact same oil inside, but the outside label showcases different uses.

Common Uses: Vitality – supports immunity and respiratory systems. Normal – calms moods, supports meditation, and enhances skin smoothing.

Best Practice: Vitality – add a drop to a capsule for daily health support. Normal – apply a drop to the back of the neck to support brain health and focus. Diffuse for a relaxing meditative experience.

LEMON

Lemon is a single species oil. It takes about 75 lemons to make one 15mL bottle of Lemon Essential Oil. It is cold pressed from the rind rather than steam distilled. Young Living offers Lemon in the normal line as well as the Vitality line for consumption, but they are the exact same oil inside the bottles.

Common Uses: Vitality – immunity, digestive, respiratory, helps flush your renal system. Normal – uplifting, dissolver, brightener.

Best Practice: Vitality – place a drop in your glass or stainless steel water bottle for a refreshing boost to your systems. Normal – diffuse for an uplifting aroma. Apply to nail beds and rub in to support nail strength. Apply a drop to a greasy spot to dissolve.

The Oil Basics

THE TOP 12 ESSENTIAL OILS & THEIR USES

PEPPERMINT Peppermint is a single species oil. It takes about one pound of peppermint material to produce one 15mL bottle of Peppermint Essential Oil. It is a natural hybrid of the spearmint and watermint species. It is offered both in the normal and Vitality line through Young Living. They are the exact same oil inside, but the outside label showcases different uses.

Common Uses: Vitality – circulatory and digestive support, airway support, cravings and appetite support. Normal – uplifting and energizing aroma, cooling sensation for topical use.

Best Practice: Vitality – add a drop to your glass or stainless steel water bottle for a refreshing experience. Add a drop to a capsule topped off with carrier oil to help support digestion and circulation. Normal – rub a drop on location with carrier oil after a strenuous workout. Apply a drop with carrier oil on temples and back of neck for a soothing cooling sensation.

CITRUS FRESH™ This energizing blend fills the whole room with an amazing aroma! The uplifting scent of blended citrus oils with a touch of Spearmint makes this synergy a family favorite. Young Living offers Lemon in the normal line as well as the Vitality line for consumption, but they are the exact same oil inside the bottles.

Common Uses: Vitality – immunity, digestive, respiratory, helps flush your systems. Normal – uplifting, clarity, dissolver, brightener.

Best Practice: Vitality – place a drop in your glass or stainless steel water bottle for a refreshing boost to your systems. Normal – diffuse to freshen the room, for an uplifting aroma, and for clarity of mind. Apply as your signature perfume. Add a drop in your night cleansing and moisturizing routine.

Essential Oil Singles in this Blend: Orange, Tangerine, Grapefruit, Lemon, Mandarin, and Spearmint.

THIEVES®
Thieves® comes from a legend about four thieves who rubbed on a similar blend before they robbed the dead and dying during the plague. It is offered both in the normal and Vitality line through Young Living. They are the exact same oil inside, but the outside label showcases different uses.

Common Uses: Vitality – immunity and cleansing support. Normal – amazing fresh aroma, helps freshen the room.

Best Practice: Vitality – add a drop to Ningxia Red® or add a drop to a capsule for a healthful morning routine. Normal – massage a drop to the bottom of the feet to support fresh smelling feet. Diffuse to keep air smelling clean and fresh.

Essential Oil Singles in this Blend: Clove, Lemon, Cinnamon Bark, Eucalyptus radiata, and Rosemary.

DIGIZE™
DiGize™ is known for its ability to soothe and relax your body. Digize Vitality™ is specifically designed to support digestive health. Aromatically it can be used to freshen the air and calm the environment.

Common Uses: Vitality – digestive support and intestinal support. Normal – calming and cleansing.

Best Practice: Vitality – Add a drop under the tongue to support systems. Add 2 drops to a capsule with carrier oil to support digestion. Normal – rub a drop on the abdomen for a soothing sensation.

Essential Oil Singles in this Blend: Tarragon, Ginger, Peppermint, Juiper, Fennel, Lemongrass, Anise, and Patchouli.

RAVEN™
Raven™ is a cleansing and opening blend that creates a cooling sensation when applied topically to the chest and throat. Raven™ calms and soothes for overall wellness. Use with carrier oil.

Common Uses: Calming, cooling, and opening for healthy breathing.

Best Practice: Rub a drop on your chest or diffuse for a calming and relaxing environment.

Essential Oil Singles in this Blend: Camphor, Lemon, Wintergreen, Peppermint, and Eucalyptus radiata.

PANAWAY®
When a person physically needs PanAway®, they usually smell it and love it! PanAway® has a minty fresh aroma and feels cool when applied topically. Use with carrier oil if needed.

Common Uses: Apply this oil with carrier oil for a refreshing after-workout experience.

Best Practice: This blend is best used topically. Apply on location liberally as needed. It is a hot oil, so it is best to use with a carrier oil.

Essential Oil Singles in this Blend: Wintergreen, Helichrysum, Clove, and Peppermint.

STRESS AWAY™

Stress Away™ is a customer favorite, and it's commonly joked that users would bathe in it if they could. It contains a small amount of Vanilla absolute, making it a favorite among everyone.

Common Uses: Calming for emotions, helpful during times of stress, great for focus and mental clarity.

Best Practice: Rub a drop on the wrists and back of neck in the morning for a more focus-friendly day. Add 6 drops to a cold water diffuser at night to calm the environment for a more restful night's sleep.

Essential Oil Singles in this Blend: Copaiba, Lime, Cedarwood, Lavender, Ocotea, and Vanilla absolute extract.

VALOR®

Valor®, also known as the "Courage Blend" is one of the most popular Young Living blends. This blend is often referred to as a "Chiropractor in a bottle." It is the foundation blend for the Raindrop Technique®. This blend helps calm and ground you.

Common Uses: Topical and Aromatic – Helpful to calm and focus the mind when diffused or applied topically. Calming and grounding to the mind, body, and soul.

Best Practice: Topical – Apply topically to the back of the neck and temples to promote clarity. Rub a drop on your wrists and forehead before bedtime or before entering a stressful situation. Add a drop directly into your belly button just before bed. Put a cotton ball over your belly button and tape in place so you do not stain your sheets.

Essential Oil Singles in this Blend: Northern Lights Black Spruce™, Camphor, Blue Tansy, Frankincense, Geranium, and Caprylic/capric triglyceride (coconut oil and glycerin).

PEACE & CALMING®

Peace & Calming® is a new mother's best friend. This blend helps littles at bedtime, but is also the perfect choice for adults, too. The gentle and sweet aroma will quickly become one of your household staples.

Common Uses: Topical and Aromatic – Helpful to relax and calm down when diffused or applied topically. Helps to soothe muscle tension and emotional needs.

Best Practice: Aromatic – Use 4 drops in your cold-water diffuser and diffuse day or night. Add a few drops to a warm bath for a relaxing experience. Topical – Rub a drop on the back of the neck, wrists, and temples to promote calming clarity and cognitive wellness and health. Rub a drop on your big toes before bed for a more restful night's sleep. Rub a drop on sore muscles after a workout.

Essential Oil Singles in this Blend: Tangerine, Orange, Ylang Ylang, Patchouli, and Blue Tansy.

The Recipes

THE BEST RECIPES FOR MAKE & TAKES

Setting up an Essential Oil 101 class may be hard enough for some people, let alone hosting a Make & Take. The best thing to remember when hosting any essential oil class is to make it simple and fun. Don't go overboard. You want your guests to have fun and think to themselves, "Wow, I could do something like this!" The pitfall with Make & Take classes is our desire to over-produce it. Resist this urge at all costs! Make & Takes can be very expensive with little return on investment. Potential customers come to the class, make several items, and go home with free or very inexpensive oil products with a justification that they want to try them before they become a member. It is far better to host an Oil 101 class with one simple Make & Take project. You can charge $5 for the item or include it as a gift for the guests. They should be very easy to make (take less than 15 minutes, and should cost you no more than $2 each with supplies and oils). The following are some great ideas for easy and cost effective projects to do for your classes, plus they make an added bonus in helping fill your classes! See more recipes in the book, *Essential Oil Make & Takes* by Jen O'Sullivan or head over to www.31oils.com/100gifts and you can get recommendations for all your supplies at www.31oils.com/supplies.

BATH SALTS
Ingredients:
- 8 ounce Glass Jar
- 1 ¾ cups Epsom Salt
- ¼ cup Baking Soda
- 8-10 drops of one of the following: Lavender , Stress Away™, Peace & Calming®, or Valor®.

DIY Directions: *Combine Salt and Baking Soda in jar, add essential oils, place lid on tightly, and shake to disperse. Decorate with ribbon and a label.*
Directions for Use: *Pour entire contents into a warm bath and enjoy!*

FACE SERUM

Ingredients:
- 10mL Dropper Bottle
- Organic Raw Grapeseed Oil
- 8-10 drops each of Lavender and Frankincense
- 1-2 drops Valor® (optional for blemish prone skin)

DIY Directions: *Combine the essential oils in the dropper bottle. Swirl to blend the two oils. Add Grapeseed oil to about ¾ full leaving room for the dropper. Fasten the dropper cap on, then swirl the bottle to blend well. Add a label that says "Deluxe Face Serum." This one is a customer favorite!*

Directions for Use: *Apply a dime-size amount (about 8 drops) all over freshly-washed face, neck, and back of hands both morning and night.*

ROLLERBALLS

Ingredients:
- One 5mL Rollerball
- V-6™ Vegetable Oil Complex (or carrier oil of choice)
- 8 drops Essential Oil Recipe of Choice

Create one of the following combos or create your own:
- Calming Support: 6 drops Stress Away™, 2 drops Frankincense
- Shoulder Massage: 4 drops each PanAway® and Lavender
- Breathe Support: 4 drops each Lavender, Lemon, and Peppermint

DIY Directions: *Add Carrier oil to the 5mL rollerball to almost full. Add essential oils. Use washi tape or make cute labels for each.*

Directions for Use: *Apply the Calming Support Roller to the back of the neck, along the spine, on the wrists, or on the big toes. Apply the Shoulder Massage Roller over the shoulder area and massage in. Apply the Breathe Support Roller on the skull behind the ears and down both jaw-lines.*

ROOM FRESHENER

Ingredients:
- 4 ounce Glass Spray Bottle
- 2 ounces Distilled Water
- 2 ounces Witch Hazel
- 8-10 drops of Lavender or Citrus Fresh™ (or Essential Oil of choice)

DIY Directions: *Fill bottle with distilled water and witch hazel, then add essential oils and shake to blend. Add a cute label. For a kid's room spritzer, use Stress Away™ for bedtime calming with a fun label called "Monster Spray Away" and for smelly rooms use a few drops of Raven® for a "Fresh Room Spray."*

Directions for Use: *Spray in the air as needed..*

HOW TO CREATE A CUSTOM STARTER KIT

Creating the right Custom Starter Kit is fun and easy. There is no actual "Custom Kit" through Young Living, so these are your instructions on how to create this for your new customer. The best strategy is to work smarter, not harder. To do this, simply combine Young Living promos. The Premium Starter Kit is the main promo. You get over 400 worth of product for $165. If the customer spends an additional 200PV worth of product before they check out, their total order will be at 300PV or $365. They will get $248 extra product for $200 plus Young Living will send them the current 300PV promo, which is usually around $150-200+ in retail value. Add your $25 bonus, and they are getting the absolute best value for their money! This gets them over $850 worth of product for only $365 plus tax and shipping, depending on the monthly promos. The best part is, this is a *customizable* Premium Starter Kit. You You will want to sign your new customer up for ER to get this deal, but let them know it is easy to cancel next month if they do not want to order. Change your perspective and change your passion. Creating a Custom Premium Starter Kit is seriously the absolute BEST value. Once you understand this and get excited about it, you will sell these all the time. It is the right thing, not only for your customer, but also for you to be able to maximize your time. Spend more time with one customer than less time with three.

OVER 60% SAVINGS!

CUSTOM KIT	PV TOTAL	WHOLESALE COST	RETAIL VALUE
PREMIUM STARTER KIT	100PV	$165	$407
CUSTOM ADD 200PV	200PV	$200	$248
300PV BONUSES	0	FREE	~$200+
$25 GIFT	0	FREE	$25
TOTAL VALUE	300PV	WHAT THEY PAY **$365**	TOTAL VALUE **$850+**

The Custom Kit

CREATING A CUSTOM PREMIUM STARTER KIT

Below is an outline of oils you can add to create a Custom PSK. You will want to find out their needs first. Customize it based on their needs using the entire Young Living product line.

START WITH THE PREMIUM STARTER KIT

1 Dewdrop Diffuser
5mL Frankincense
5mL Lavender
5mL Lemon Vitality™
5mL Peppermint Vitality™
5mL Citrus Fresh Vitality™
5mL DiGize Vitality™

5mL PanAway®
5mL Raven™
5mL Valor®
5mL Peace & Calming®
5mL Stress Away™
5mL Thieves Vitality™
Additional PSK samples.

Add one of the following sets on ER or create your own. (Must be 200PV or more.)

VITALITY SET (201PV)

5mL Basil Vitality™
5mL Bergamot Vitality™
5mL Celery Seed Vitality™
5mL Cinnamon Bark Vitality™
5mL Clove Vitality™
5mL Dill Vitality™
5mL EndoFlex Vitality™
5mL Ginger Vitality™
5mL Grapefruit Vitality™
5mL Jade Lemon Vitality™
5mL Lemongrass Vitality™
5mL Lime Vitality™
5mL Marjoram Vitality™
5mL Orange Vitality™
5mL Oregano Vitality™
5mL Rosemary Vitality™
5mL Spearmint Vitality™
5mL Tangerine Vitality™

IMMUNITY & ENERGY (200.50PV)

NingXia Red® (2 Pack)
Inner Defense™ Capsules
Super B™
NingXia Zyng™
NingXia Nitro®
Nutmeg Vitality™

CALMING & SLEEP (208PV)

5mL Copaiba
5mL Gentle Baby™
5mL Vetiver
5mL Northern Lights Black Spruce
5mL Cedarwood
5mL KidScents SleepyIze™
Tranquil Roll-on™
ImmuPro™
Sleep Essence™

Once you add the extra 200PV to their PSK order, you will see in their shopping cart all the extras. If you want to promote this special, just change out the monthly promo by adding in the extra items. For the most exciting promo, add the 12 oils from the PSK to the Vitality Set, which has 18 oils. Then add the oils from that month's 300PV promo to total up the offer. It comes out to usually over $850 in retail value product for only $365!

A NOTE ON COMPLIANCE

The FDA regulates what distributors of an essential oil company can and cannot say to their customers to protect them from liability. The term used for this is "compliance." This is for your protection as a distributor. It may feel like you are being handcuffed, but it is important to understand the blessing that working compliantly within your business brings. Compliance may be a new concept for you since we live in a world where freedom of speech matters. Consider this simple exchange between you, a distributor of essential oils, and a friend who has not used essential oils before. Your friend has a raging migraine. She asks if you have any oil that may help. You personally have found Peppermint to work well for you, so you gladly give her some to try. A couple hours later, your friend tells you it didn't work. Just as she suspected–oils don't work and she then decides oils are a sham. The issue here is, you do not know *why* she has a migraine. It could be from hormones, or dehydration, or perhaps the 9 cups of black coffee she has consumed that day. The point is, oils do not work the same way as pharmaceuticals do. Essential oils work organically in our bodies to help support health, not cure illness. A more serious claim could land you in a lawsuit where the court may rule against you simply because there is not enough information on essential oils. The reality is, if you operate your business and disregard compliance, your account will get shut down by Young Living. It is to protect the company as a whole. If one of their distributors in overtly non-compliant, the FDA could step in and shut down the entire company. Young Living will give you a warning and will work with you to train you and help you clean up anything you are doing incorrectly. They want you to succeed, but it is best to start off on the right foot to begin with. Here are some simple tips to keep both you and your customers happy.

- *Talk about oils from a health perspective. This is called speaking "above the wellness line."*

- *Never use any words that imply or claim sickness. Examples: cough, sore throat, cold, flu, sick, under-the-weather, infection, virus, bacteria, inflammation, pain, migraine, headache, head-in-a-vice, heartburn, high blood pressure, constipation, diarrhea, depression, etc.*

- *Never use any words that are clearly diseases or names for disorders. Examples: Cancer, COPD, Diabetes, Pneumonia, Eczema, Gout, ADD/ADHD, or any autoimmune disorder such as MS, Lyme, FM, RA, etc.*

- *FDA Guidelines state that a product may not be labeled for topical and aromatic use as well as for consumption. Structure function claims, such as respiratory, digestive, or circulatory claims, are only permissible for dietary supplements. When making structure function claims, only refer to the Vitality™ line of consumable essential oils.*

- *Never share links to other websites on your own website or on any social media platform. Example: do not share a recipe from another website and link that website. It is better to copy and paste the recipe and give credit to the website name without the dot com at the end. The reason for this is if the website you link to has any non-compliant information on it at all, you are also liable.*

- *Do not give out non-compliant information to your customers at the time of sale. You may direct them to third party resources (see The Resources page) to help them in their own research or suggest they take a free course at The School for Aromatic Studies.*

- *Always remind your customers that oils help support health, not cure disease.*